SHETLAND FROM THE SEA

SHETLAND FROM THE SEA

by

DICK KOOPMANS

The Shetland Times
Lerwick
2014

Shetland from the Sea.

First published by The Shetland Times Ltd., 2014.

ISBN 978-1-904746-92-8

A catalogue record for this book is available from the British Library.

The original size of the watercolour painting in this booklet are, apart from a few small ones, 54 x 35cm.

Printed and published by
The Shetland Times Ltd.,
Gremista, Lerwick,
Shetland ZE1 0PX.

Introduction

Dutch yacht designer Dick Koopmans and his wife Elly have sailed to Shetland regularly since 1982, often direct from their home town of Lelystad in the Netherlands.

In their yacht *Jantine V* they have sailed all over the world, from the Arctic to the Antarctic, around the world via the the "Roaring Forties", and via the Panama Canal to Mexico, Alaska and the Aleutians. This resulted in more than two hundred paintings from 36 countries in oil and watercolour, all painted by Dick.

Elly published their stories in the leading Dutch watersport magazine "Waterkampioen" and wrote four books about their travels while produced the illustrations.

They love the Shetland islands and the people very much and, after their ocean crossings ended in 2002, they visit Shetland nearly every year.

Most of the watercolours in this booklet are made from sketches during walks or from their anchorages and worked out on board.

Ruin at Bressay

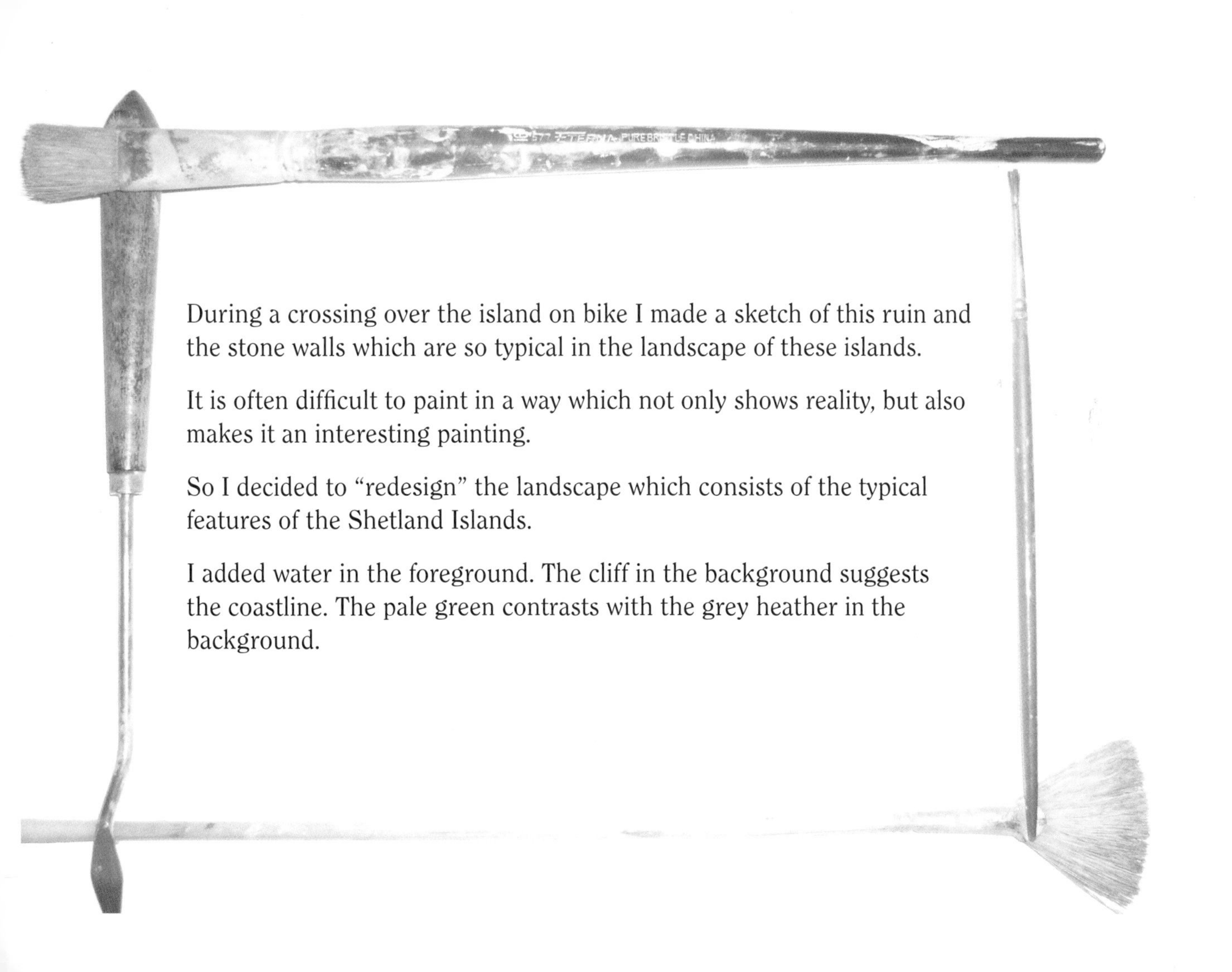

During a crossing over the island on bike I made a sketch of this ruin and the stone walls which are so typical in the landscape of these islands.

It is often difficult to paint in a way which not only shows reality, but also makes it an interesting painting.

So I decided to “redesign” the landscape which consists of the typical features of the Shetland Islands.

I added water in the foreground. The cliff in the background suggests the coastline. The pale green contrasts with the grey heather in the background.

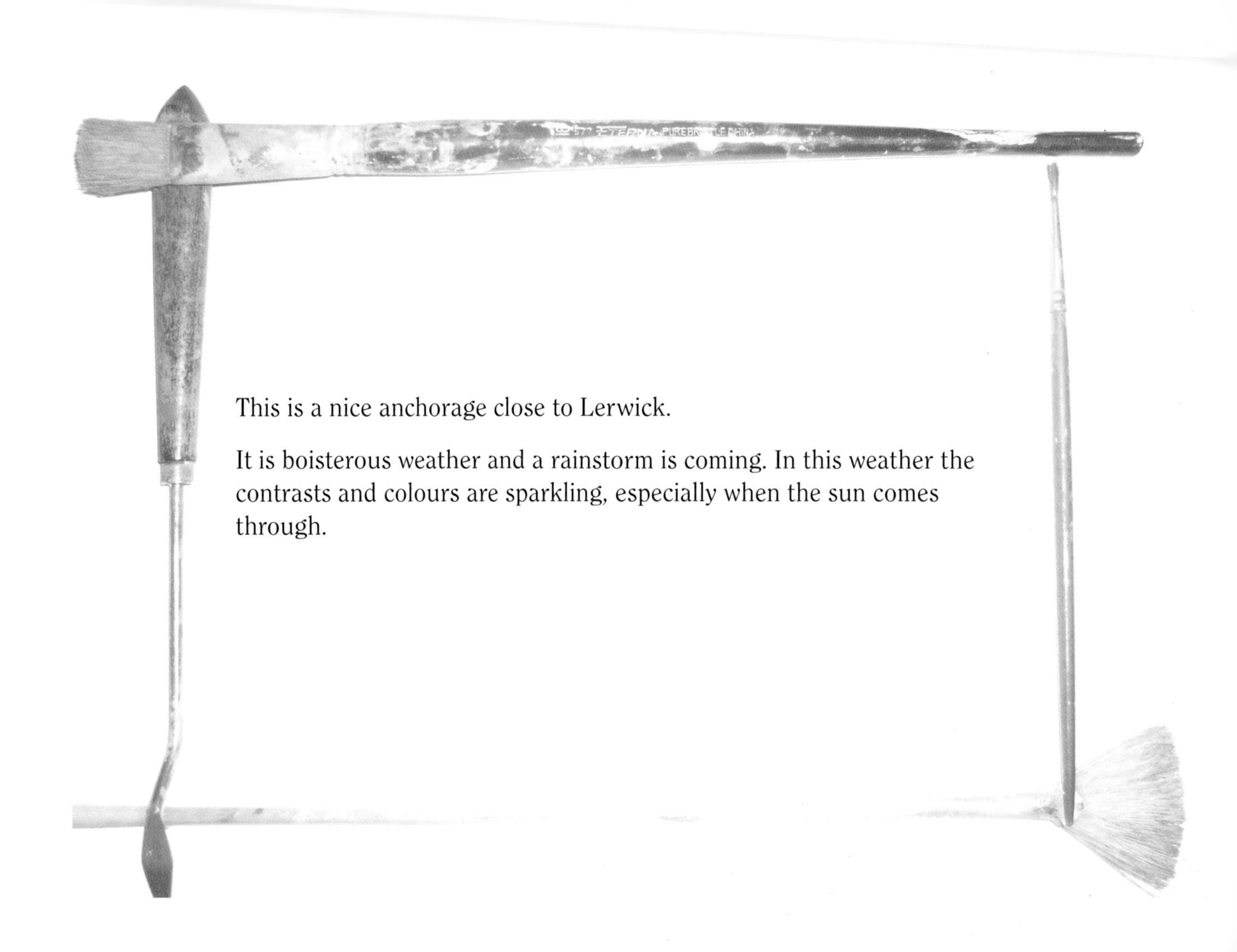

This is a nice anchorage close to Lerwick.

It is boisterous weather and a rainstorm is coming. In this weather the contrasts and colours are sparkling, especially when the sun comes through.

North Voe of Gletness

Malcolm Head - Fair Isle

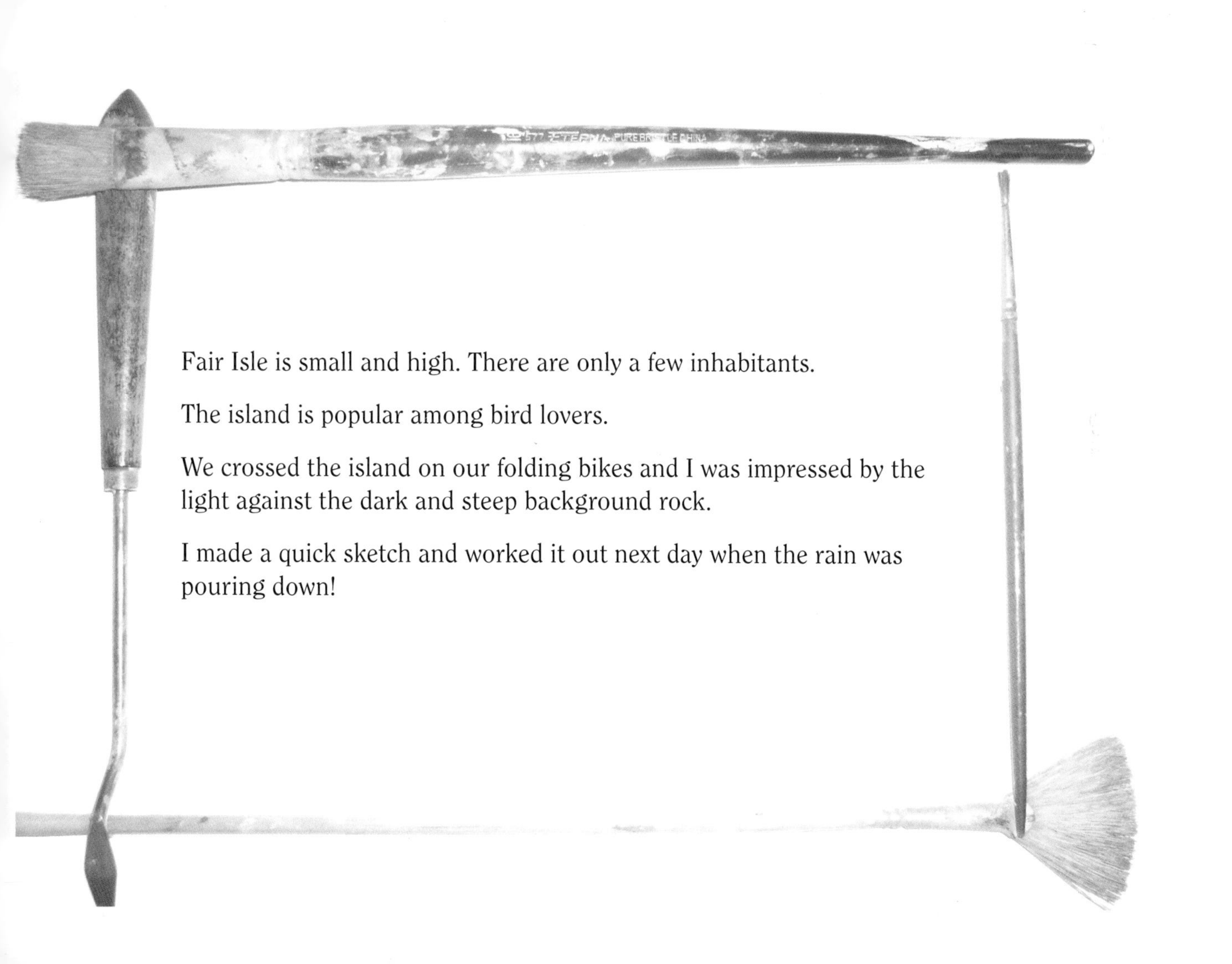

Fair Isle is small and high. There are only a few inhabitants.

The island is popular among bird lovers.

We crossed the island on our folding bikes and I was impressed by the light against the dark and steep background rock.

I made a quick sketch and worked it out next day when the rain was pouring down!

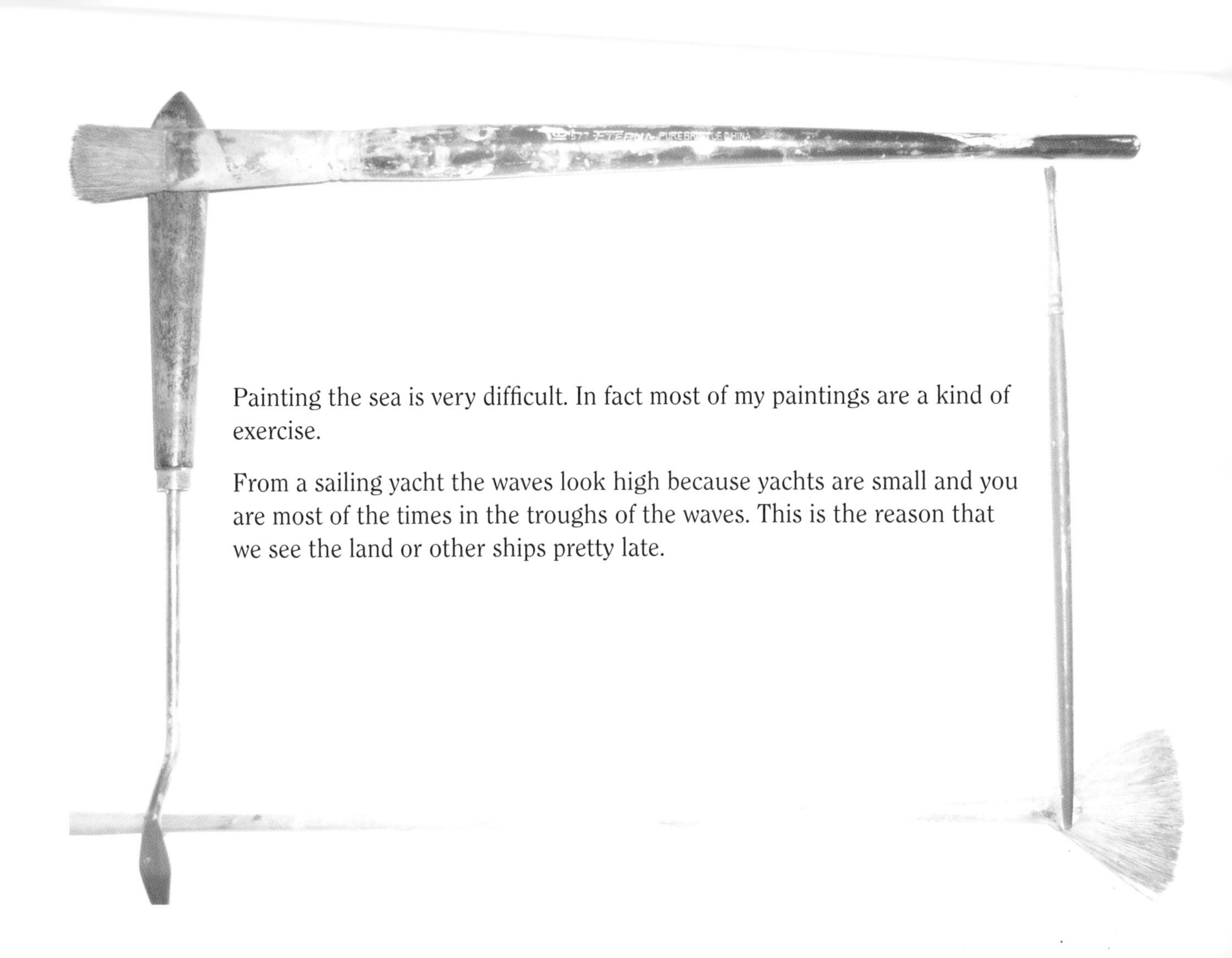

Painting the sea is very difficult. In fact most of my paintings are a kind of exercise.

From a sailing yacht the waves look high because yachts are small and you are most of the times in the troughs of the waves. This is the reason that we see the land or other ships pretty late.

Approaching the Shetland Islands

Approaching the Shetland Islands

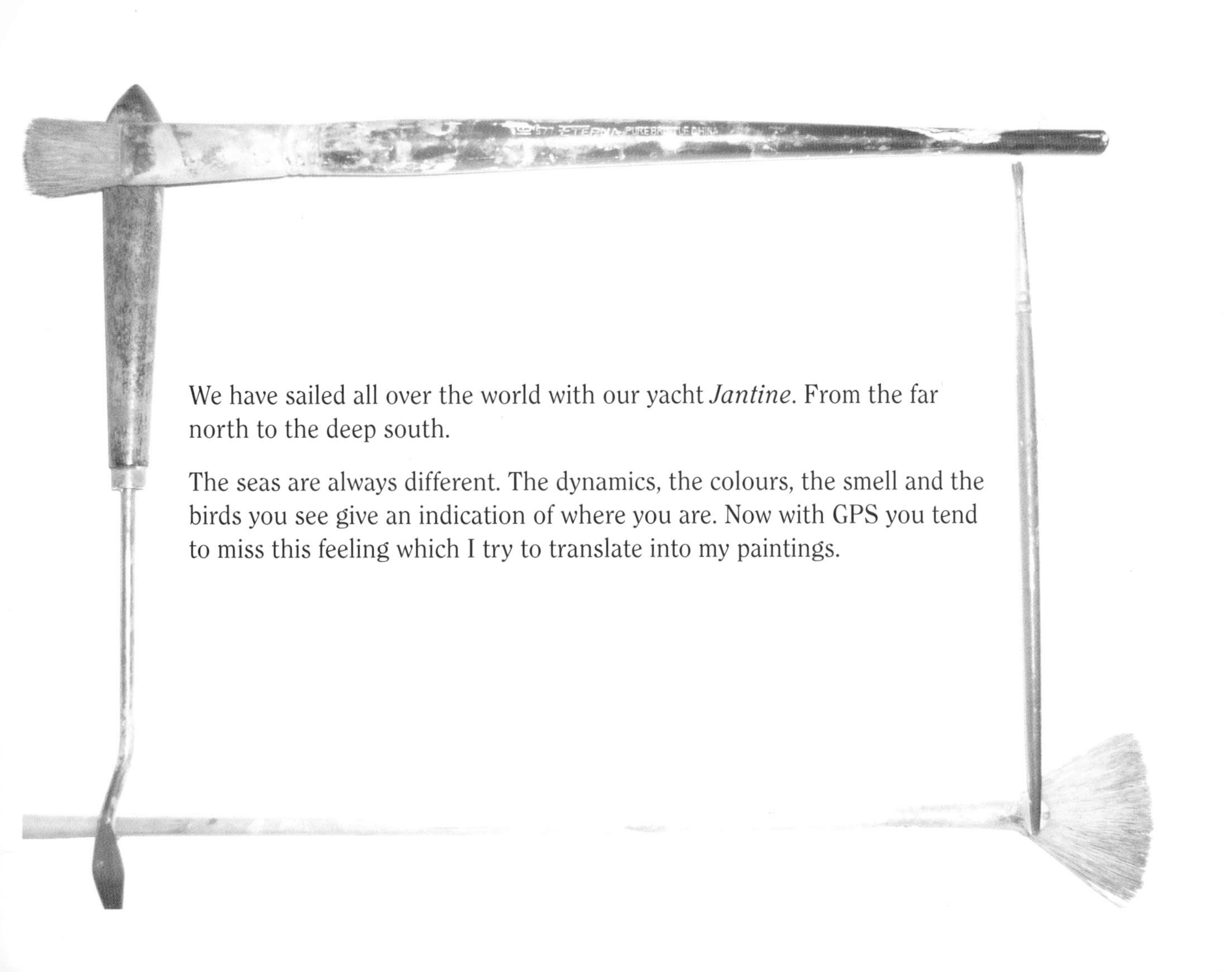

We have sailed all over the world with our yacht *Jantine*. From the far north to the deep south.

The seas are always different. The dynamics, the colours, the smell and the birds you see give an indication of where you are. Now with GPS you tend to miss this feeling which I try to translate into my paintings.

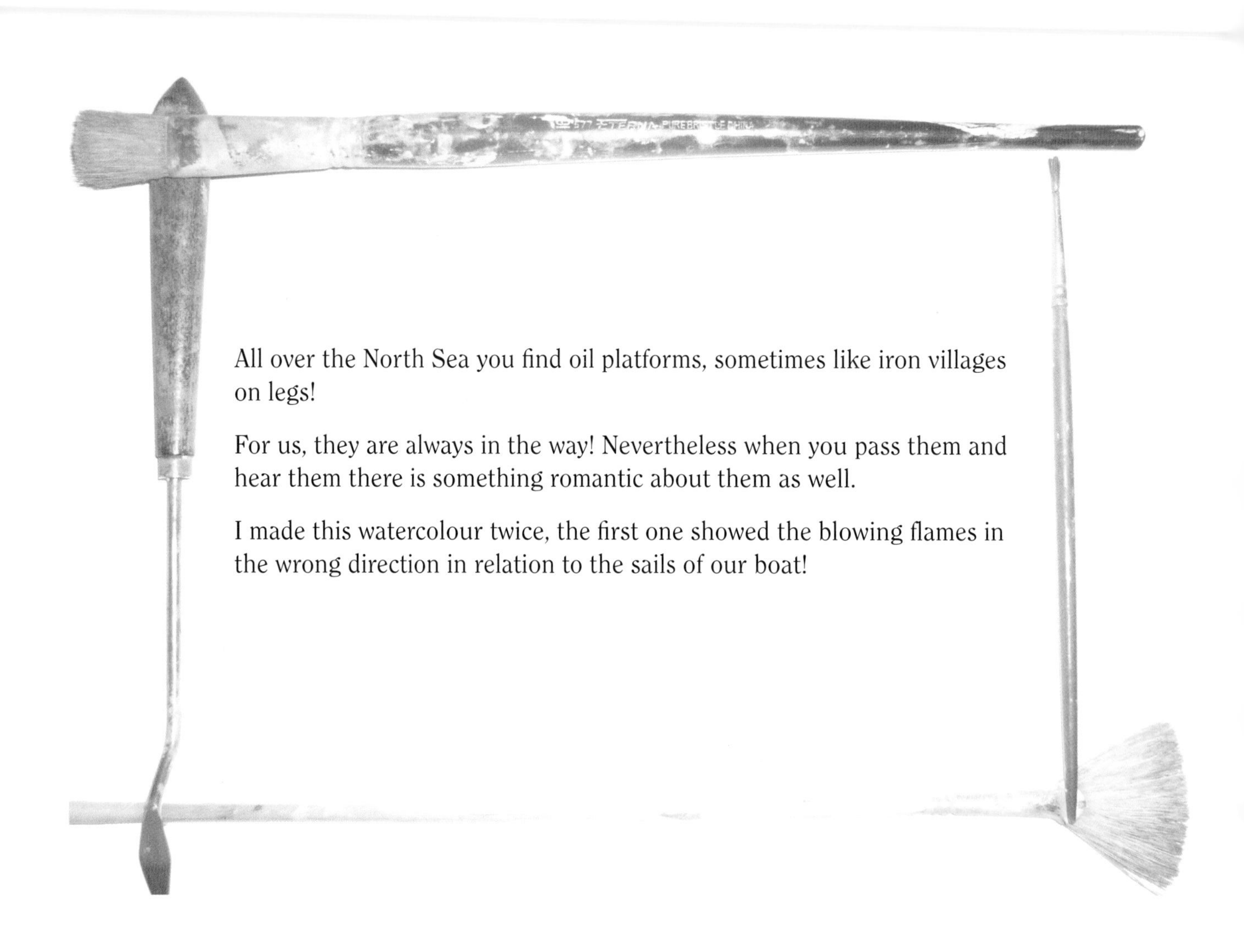

All over the North Sea you find oil platforms, sometimes like iron villages on legs!

For us, they are always in the way! Nevertheless when you pass them and hear them there is something romantic about them as well.

I made this watercolour twice, the first one showed the blowing flames in the wrong direction in relation to the sails of our boat!

Jantine passing an oil platform.

Aith Voe - Bressay

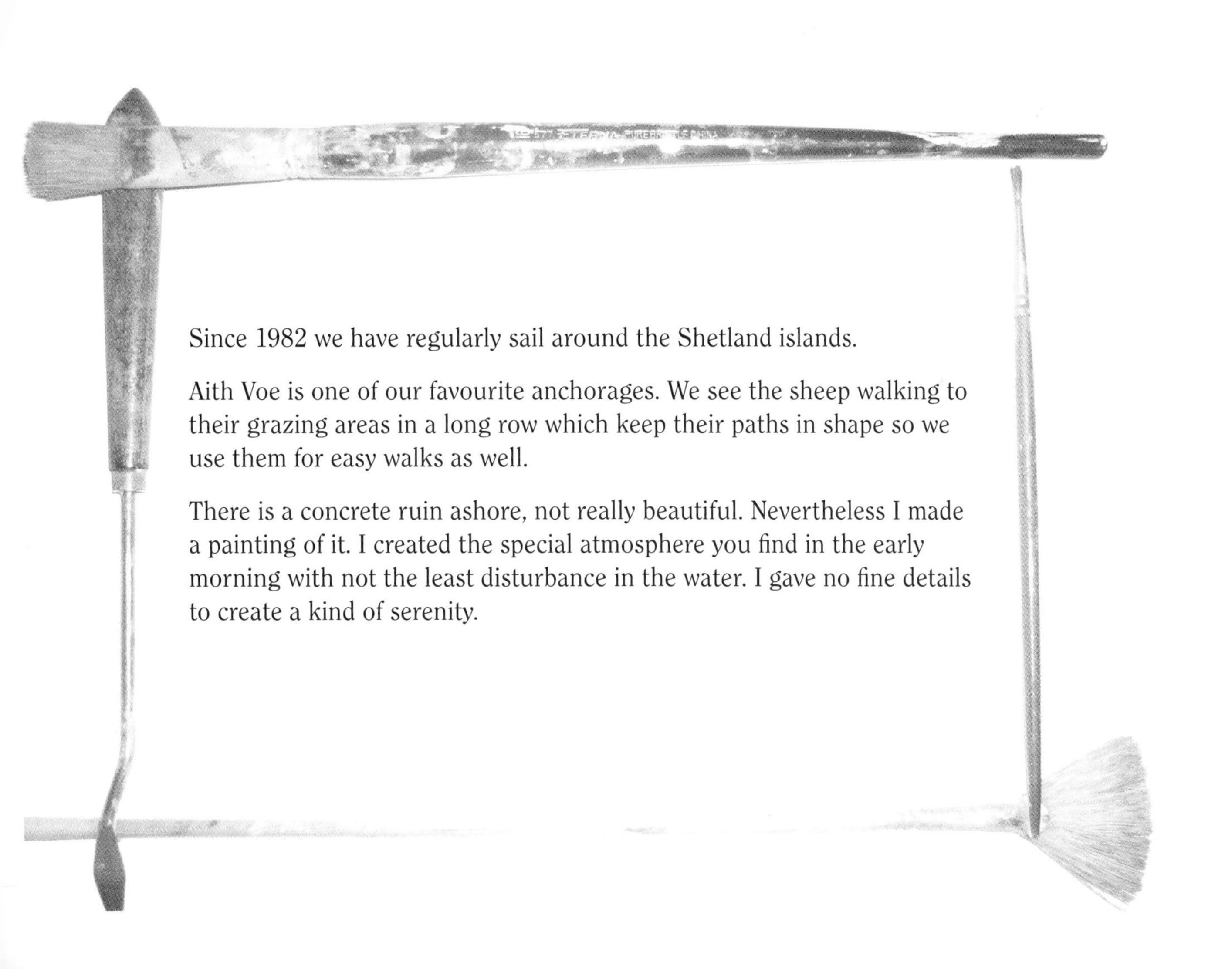

Since 1982 we have regularly sail around the Shetland islands.

Aith Voe is one of our favourite anchorages. We see the sheep walking to their grazing areas in a long row which keep their paths in shape so we use them for easy walks as well.

There is a concrete ruin ashore, not really beautiful. Nevertheless I made a painting of it. I created the special atmosphere you find in the early morning with not the least disturbance in the water. I gave no fine details to create a kind of serenity.

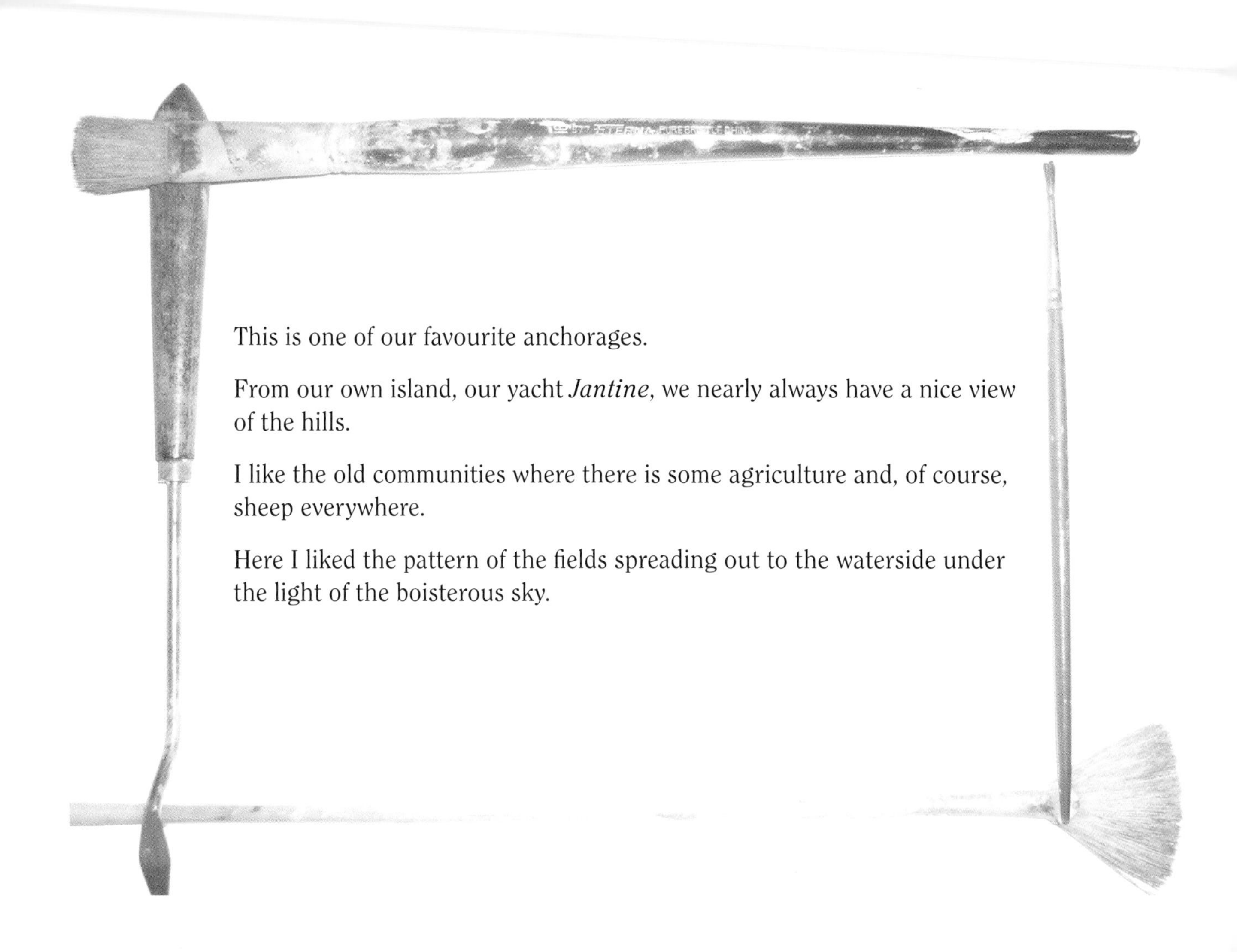

This is one of our favourite anchorages.

From our own island, our yacht *Jantine*, we nearly always have a nice view of the hills.

I like the old communities where there is some agriculture and, of course, sheep everywhere.

Here I liked the pattern of the fields spreading out to the waterside under the light of the boisterous sky.

Gunnister – Aith Voe – Bressay

Nesti Voe – Noss

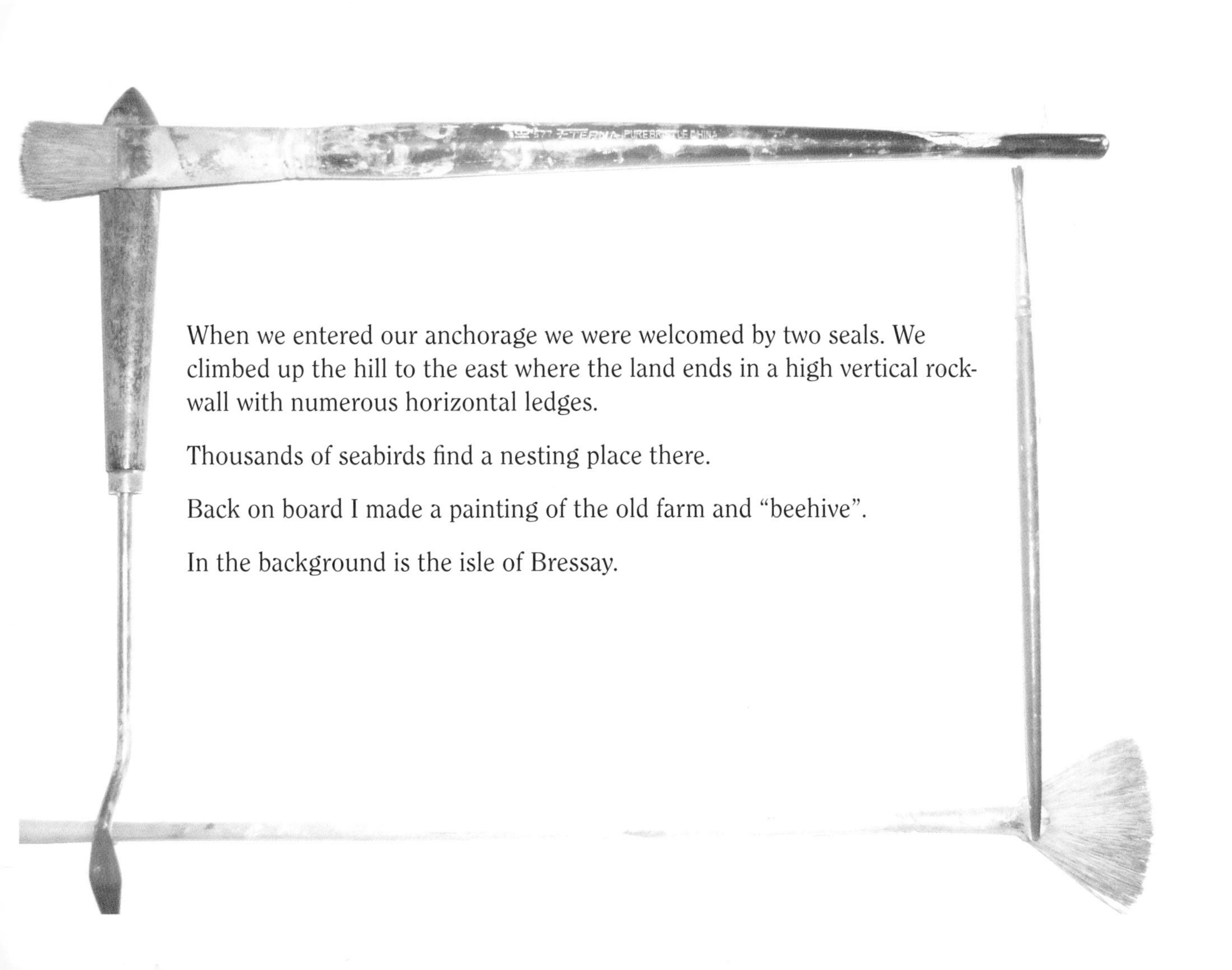

When we entered our anchorage we were welcomed by two seals. We climbed up the hill to the east where the land ends in a high vertical rock-wall with numerous horizontal ledges.

Thousands of seabirds find a nesting place there.

Back on board I made a painting of the old farm and “beehive”.

In the background is the isle of Bressay.

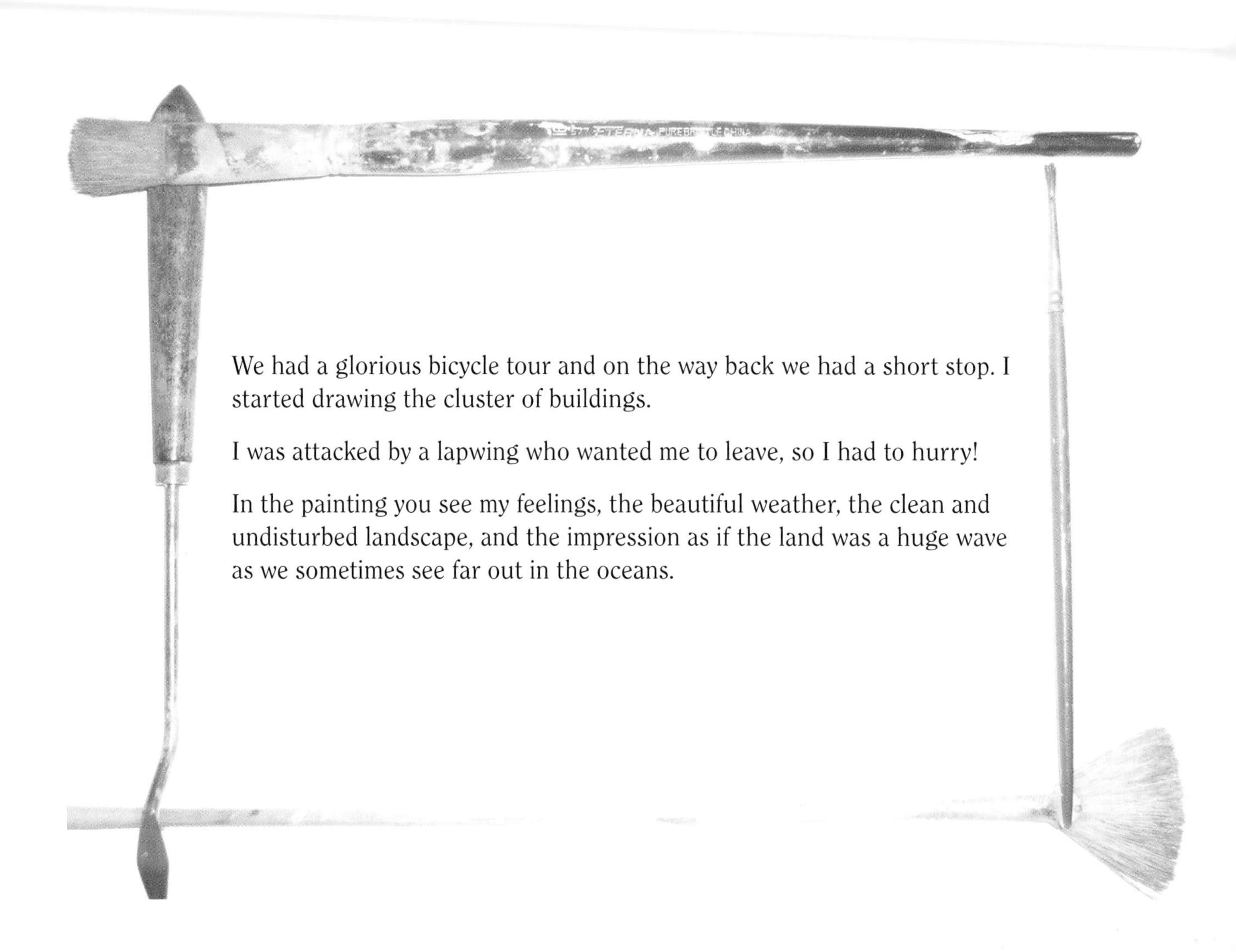

We had a glorious bicycle tour and on the way back we had a short stop. I started drawing the cluster of buildings.

I was attacked by a lapwing who wanted me to leave, so I had to hurry!

In the painting you see my feelings, the beautiful weather, the clean and undisturbed landscape, and the impression as if the land was a huge wave as we sometimes see far out in the oceans.

Burravoe - Yell

Bremen Böd - Whalsay

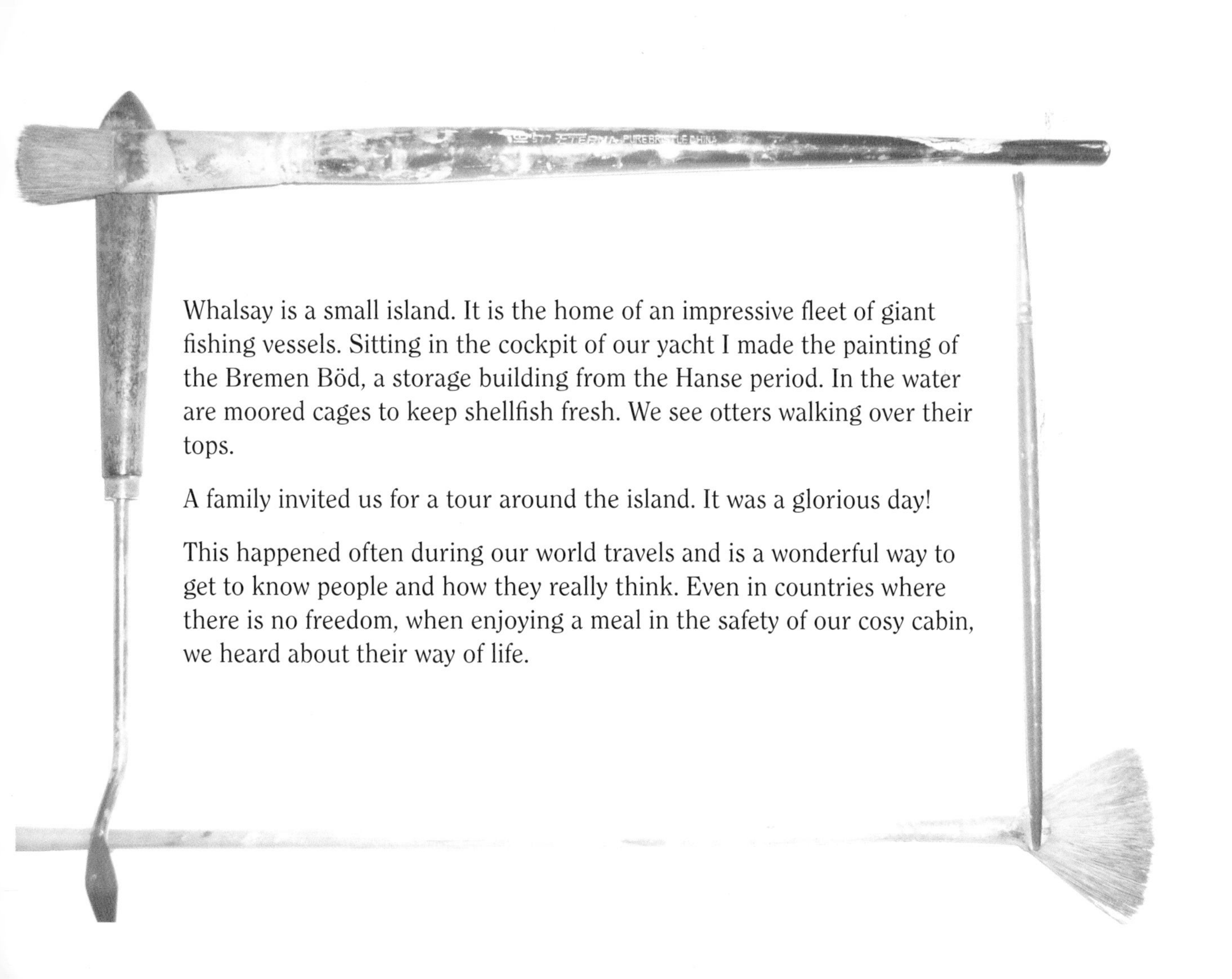

Whalsay is a small island. It is the home of an impressive fleet of giant fishing vessels. Sitting in the cockpit of our yacht I made the painting of the Bremen Böd, a storage building from the Hanse period. In the water are moored cages to keep shellfish fresh. We see otters walking over their tops.

A family invited us for a tour around the island. It was a glorious day!

This happened often during our world travels and is a wonderful way to get to know people and how they really think. Even in countries where there is no freedom, when enjoying a meal in the safety of our cosy cabin, we heard about their way of life.

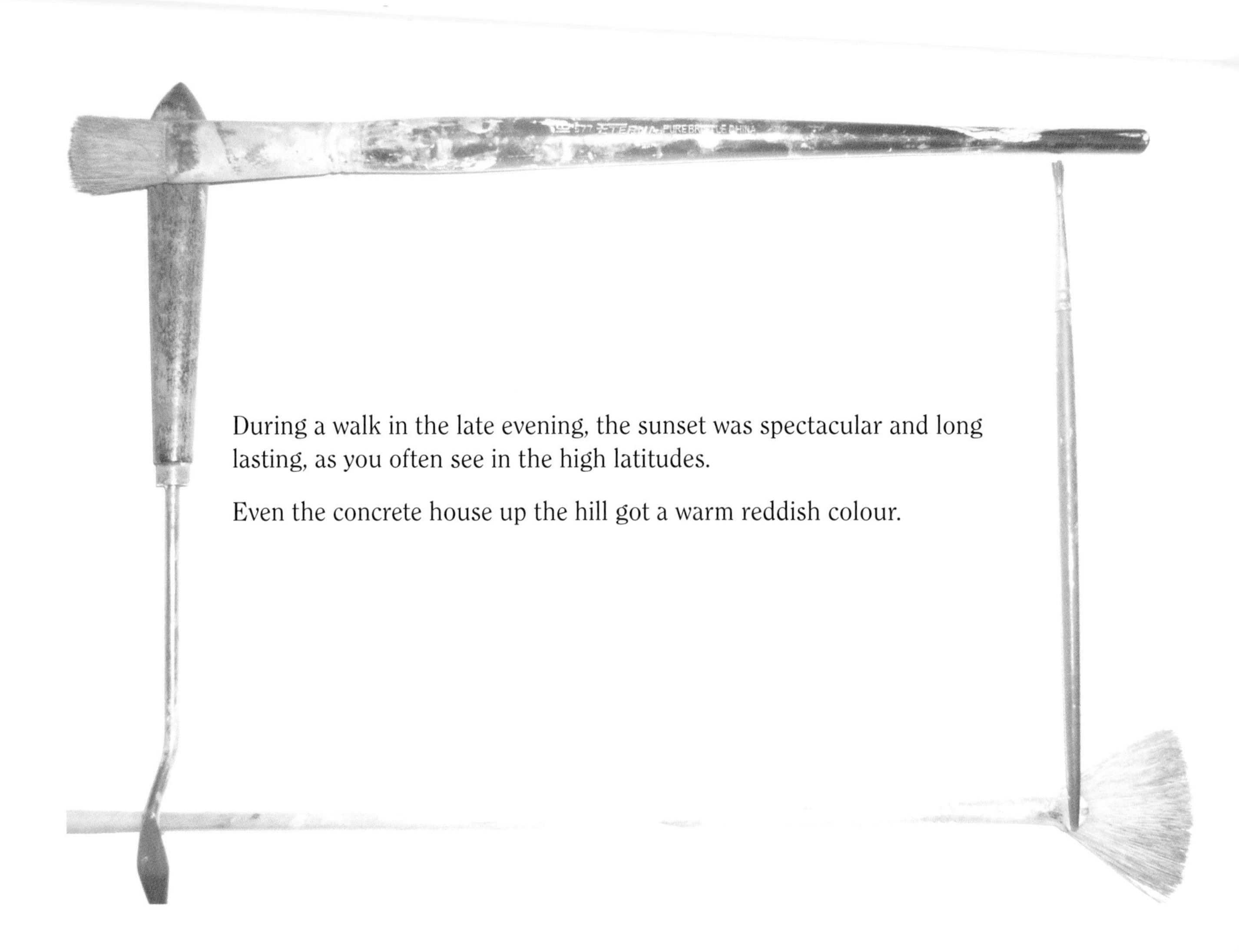

During a walk in the late evening, the sunset was spectacular and long lasting, as you often see in the high latitudes.

Even the concrete house up the hill got a warm reddish colour.

Burravoe - Yell

Buness House – Baltasound – Unst

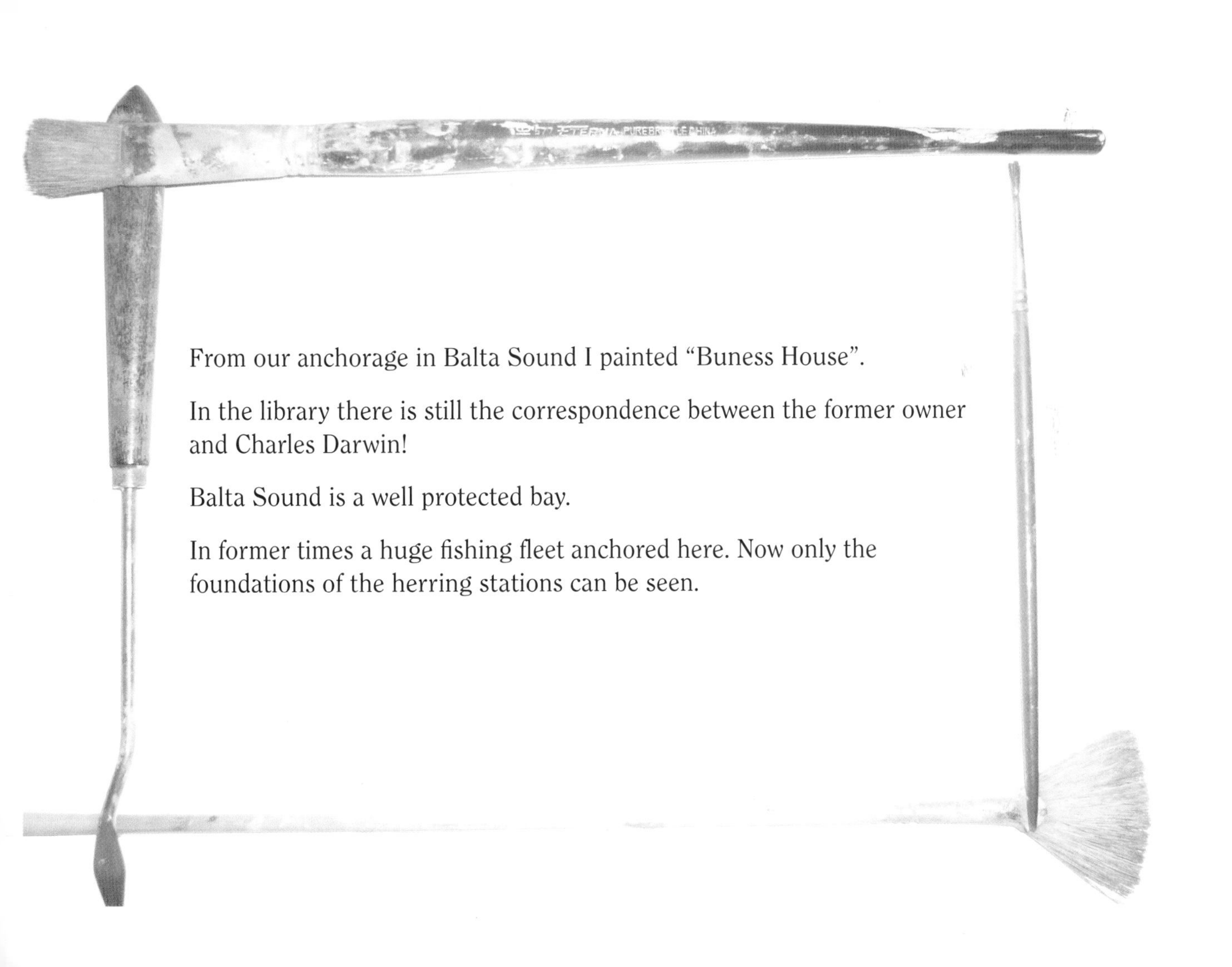

From our anchorage in Balta Sound I painted “Buness House”.

In the library there is still the correspondence between the former owner and Charles Darwin!

Balta Sound is a well protected bay.

In former times a huge fishing fleet anchored here. Now only the foundations of the herring stations can be seen.

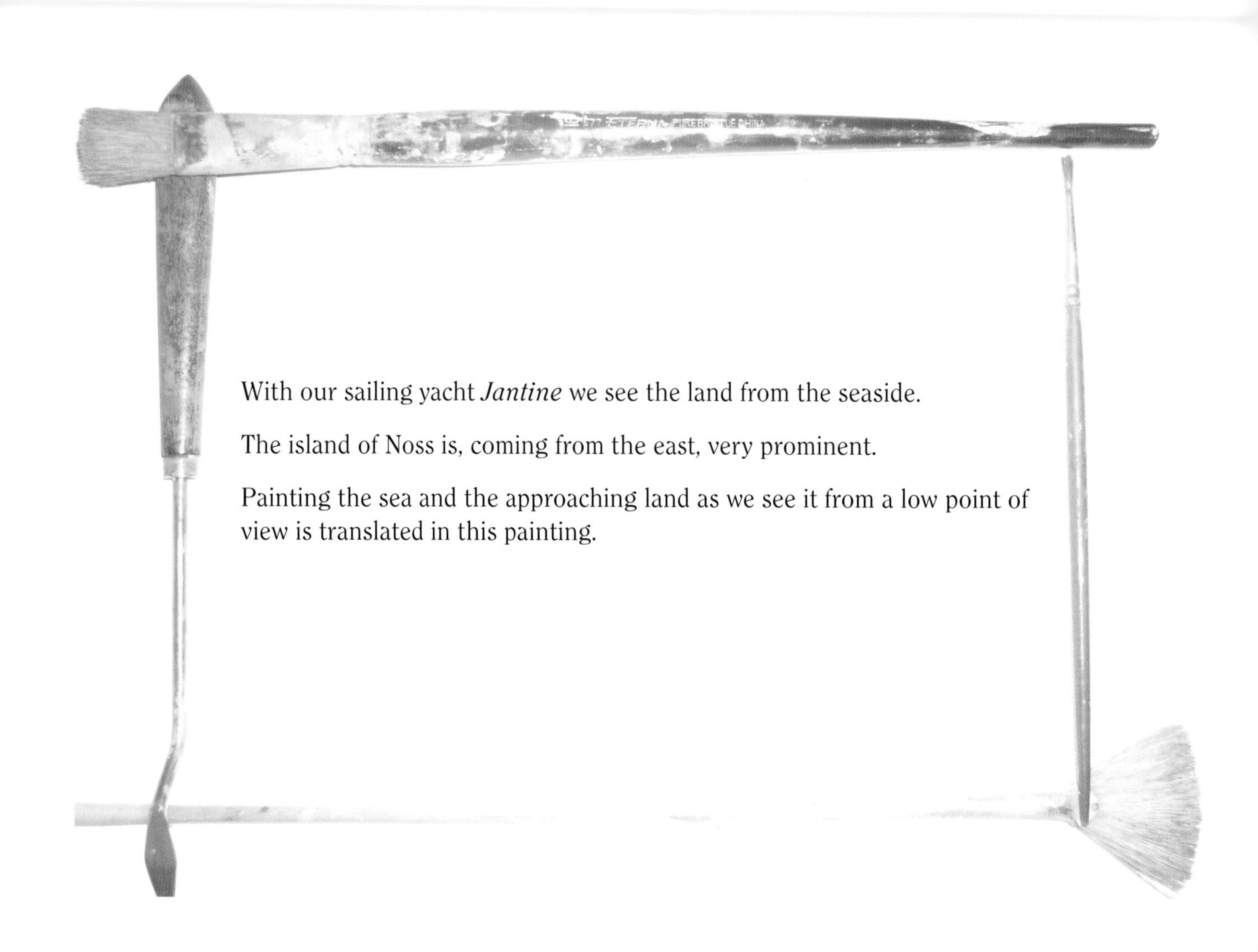

With our sailing yacht *Jantine* we see the land from the seaside.

The island of Noss is, coming from the east, very prominent.

Painting the sea and the approaching land as we see it from a low point of view is translated in this painting.

Rough seas off Noss

“Sixareen” - Unst

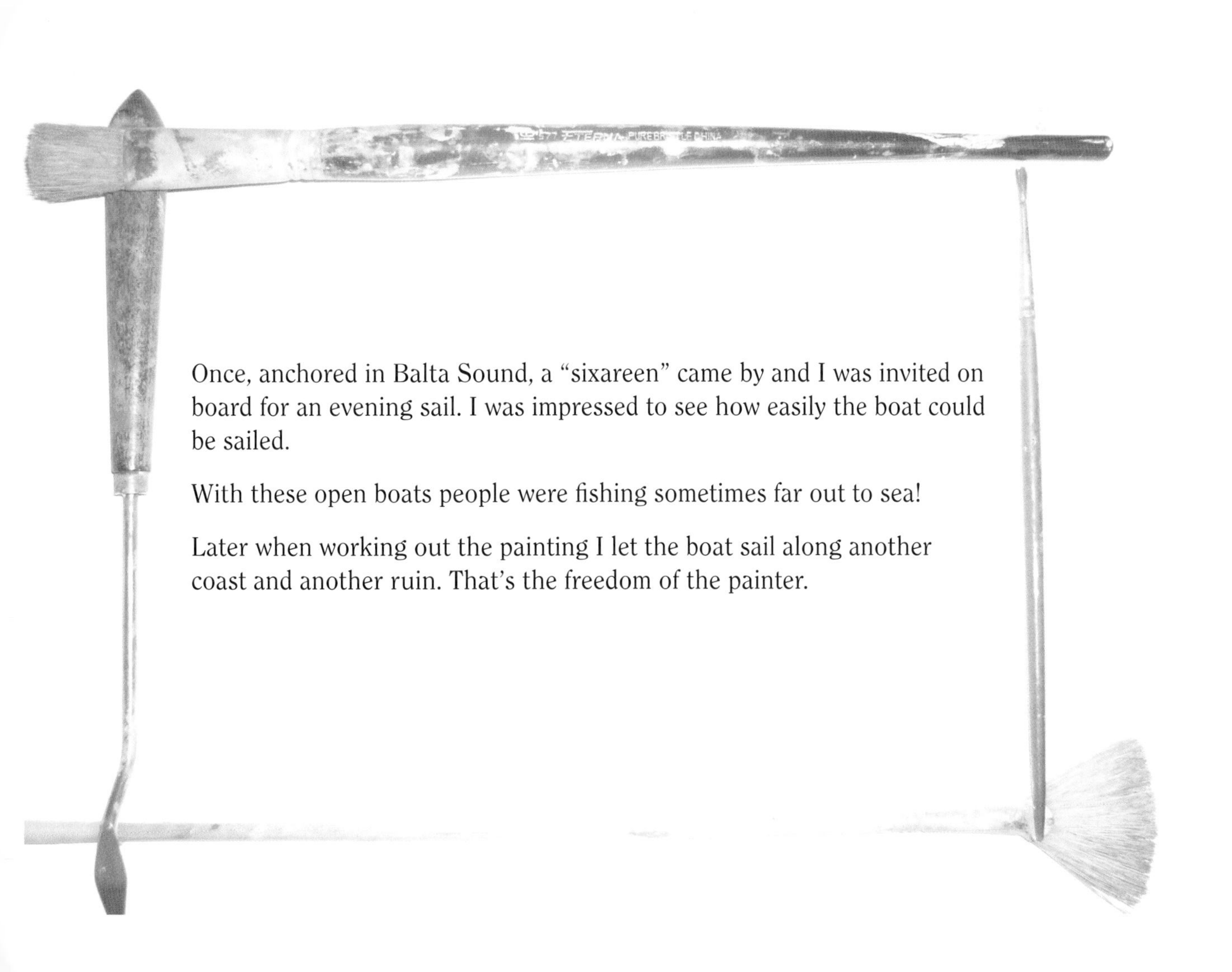

Once, anchored in Balta Sound, a “sixareen” came by and I was invited on board for an evening sail. I was impressed to see how easily the boat could be sailed.

With these open boats people were fishing sometimes far out to sea!

Later when working out the painting I let the boat sail along another coast and another ruin. That’s the freedom of the painter.

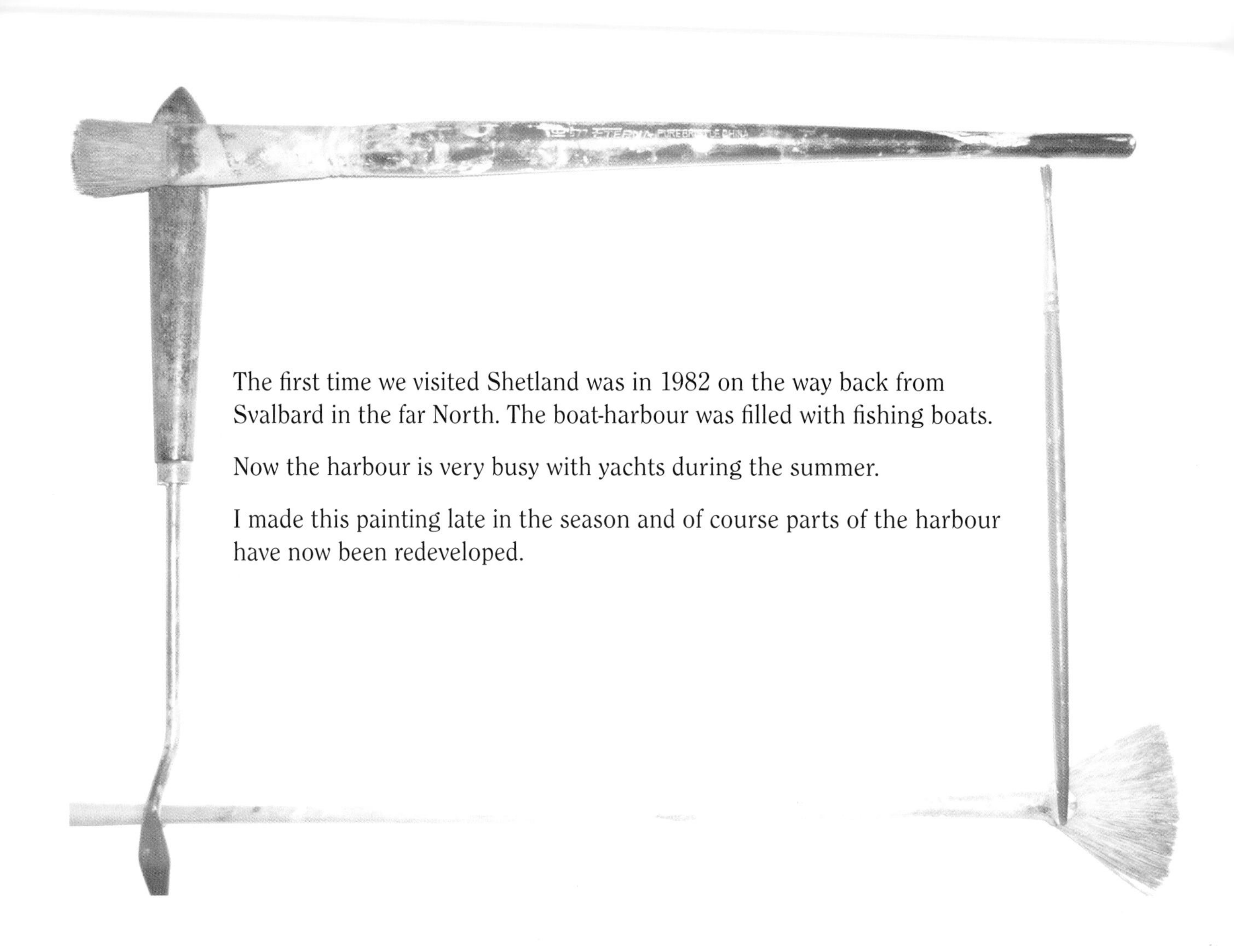

The first time we visited Shetland was in 1982 on the way back from Svalbard in the far North. The boat-harbour was filled with fishing boats.

Now the harbour is very busy with yachts during the summer.

I made this painting late in the season and of course parts of the harbour have now been redeveloped.

Boat harbour - Lerwick

Burravoe - Yell

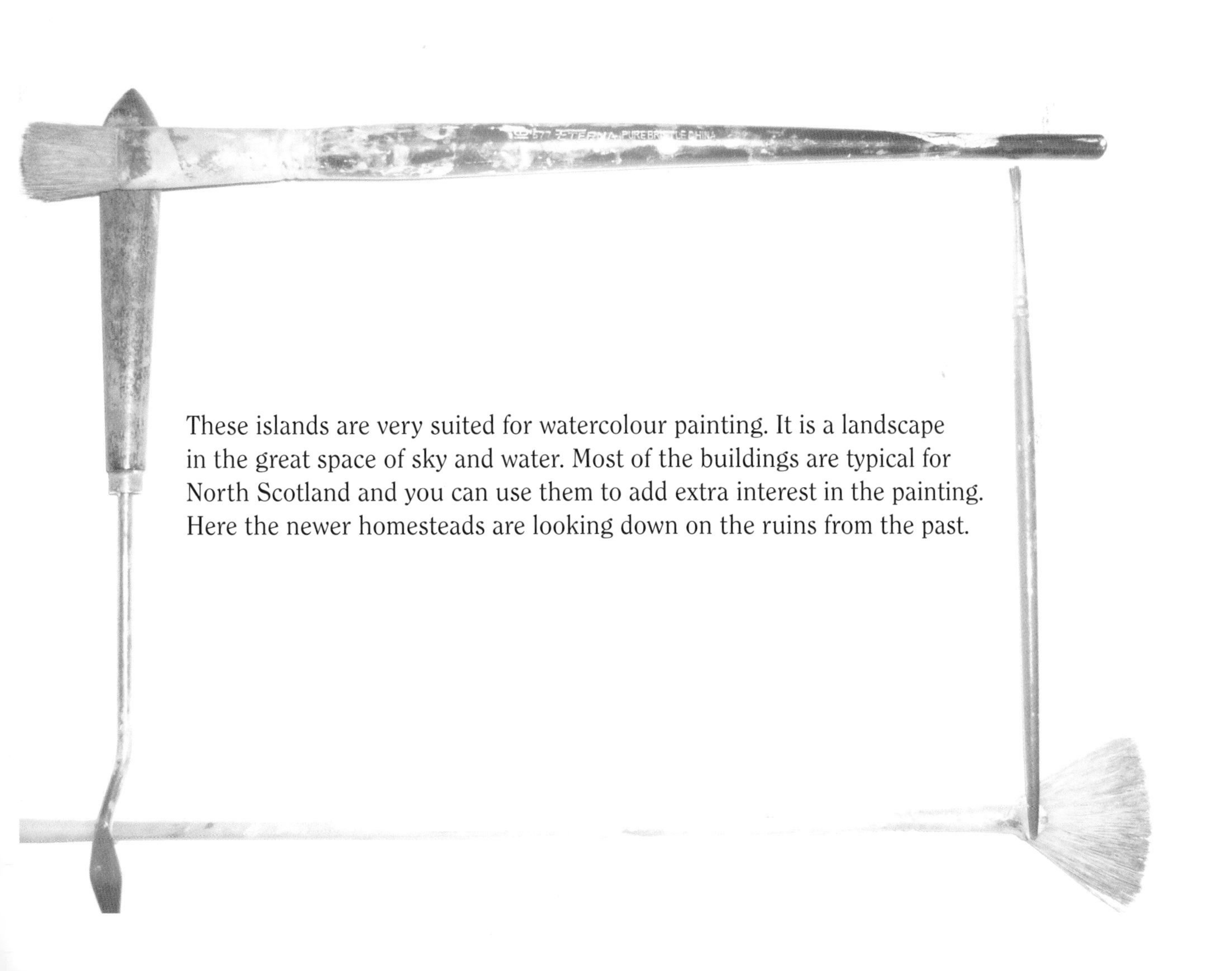

These islands are very suited for watercolour painting. It is a landscape in the great space of sky and water. Most of the buildings are typical for North Scotland and you can use them to add extra interest in the painting. Here the newer homesteads are looking down on the ruins from the past.

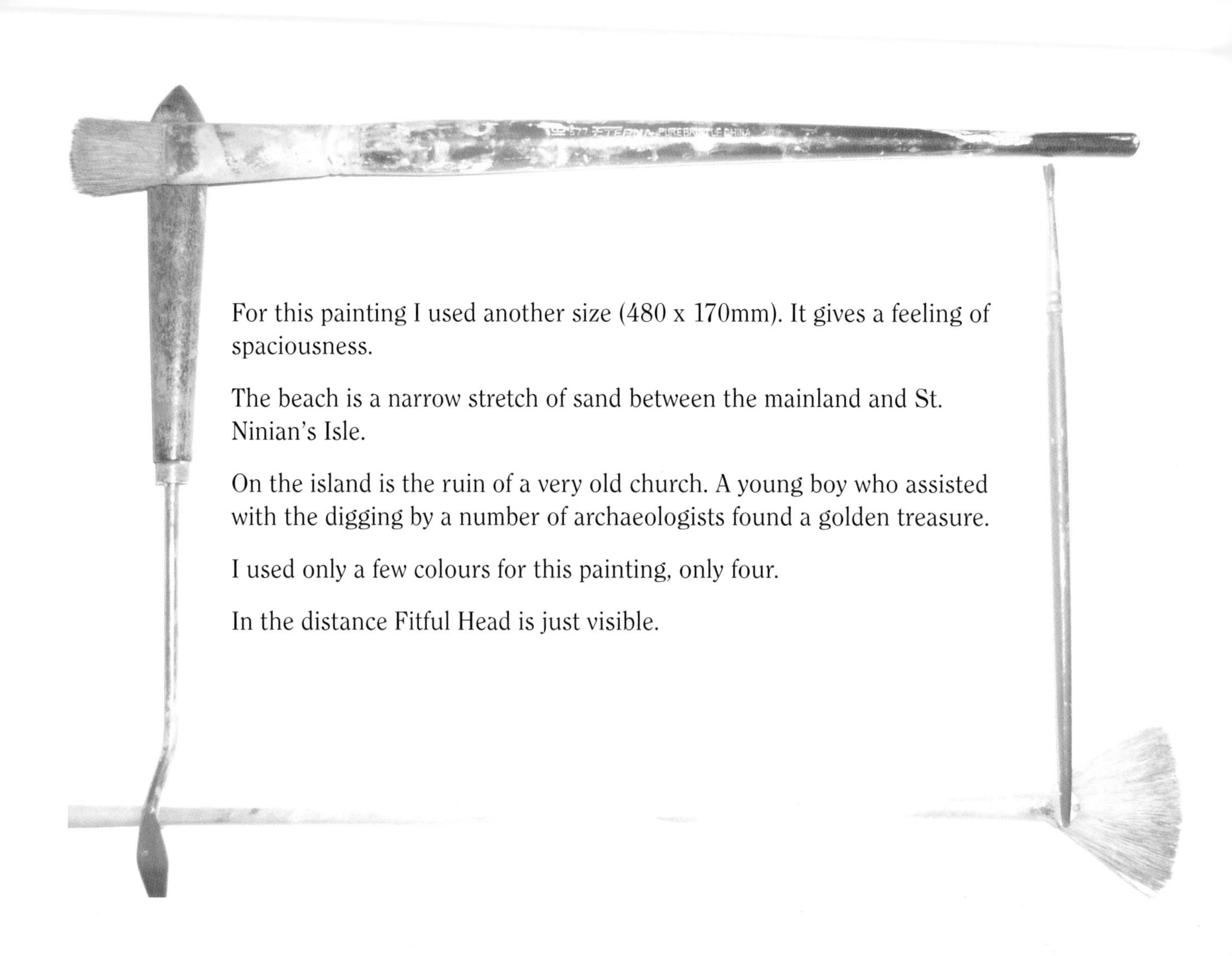

For this painting I used another size (480 x 170mm). It gives a feeling of spaciousness.

The beach is a narrow stretch of sand between the mainland and St. Ninian's Isle.

On the island is the ruin of a very old church. A young boy who assisted with the digging by a number of archaeologists found a golden treasure.

I used only a few colours for this painting, only four.

In the distance Fitful Head is just visible.

St Ninian's Isle - South Mainland

Linganess - Nesting

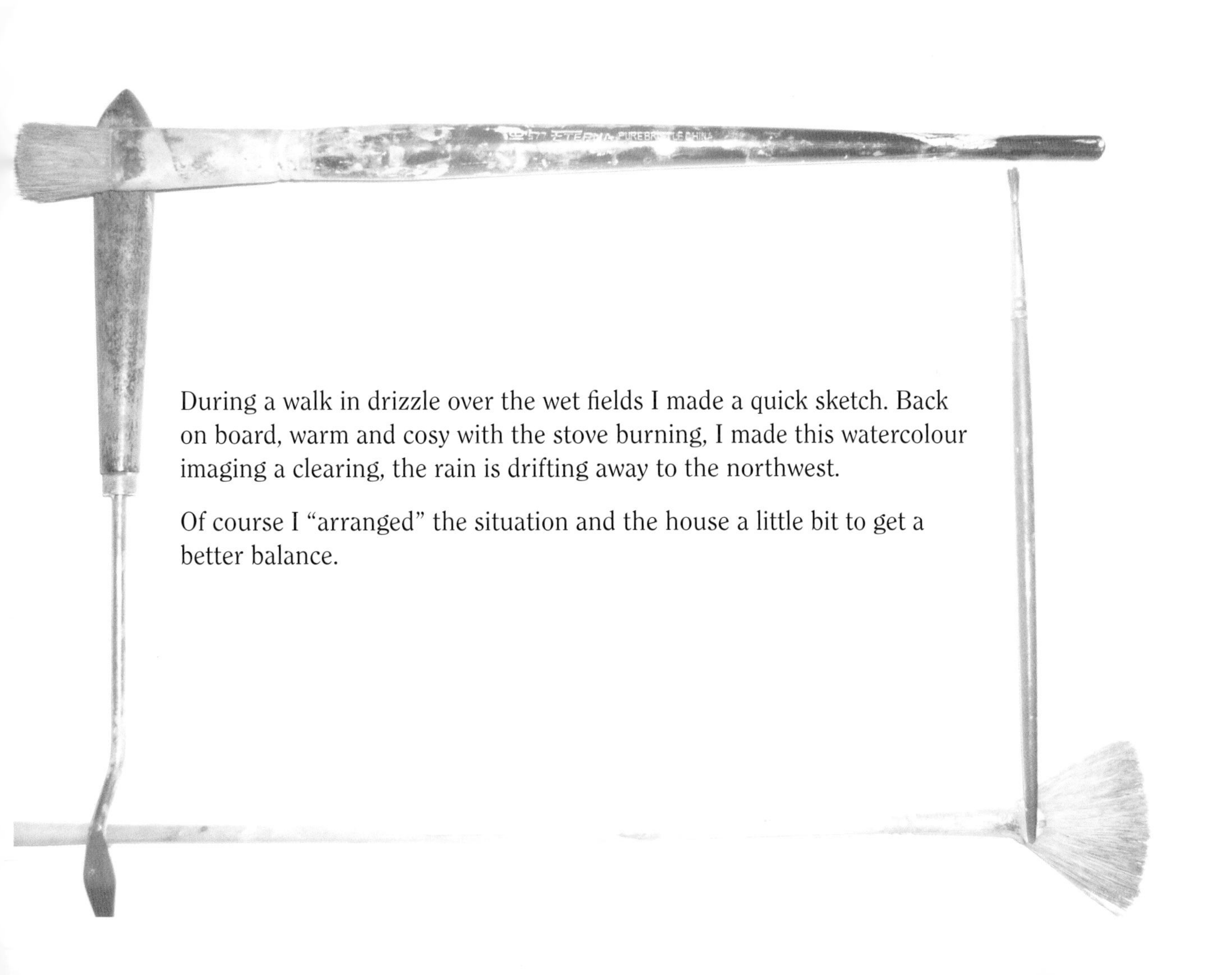

During a walk in drizzle over the wet fields I made a quick sketch. Back on board, warm and cosy with the stove burning, I made this watercolour imaging a clearing, the rain is drifting away to the northwest.

Of course I "arranged" the situation and the house a little bit to get a better balance.

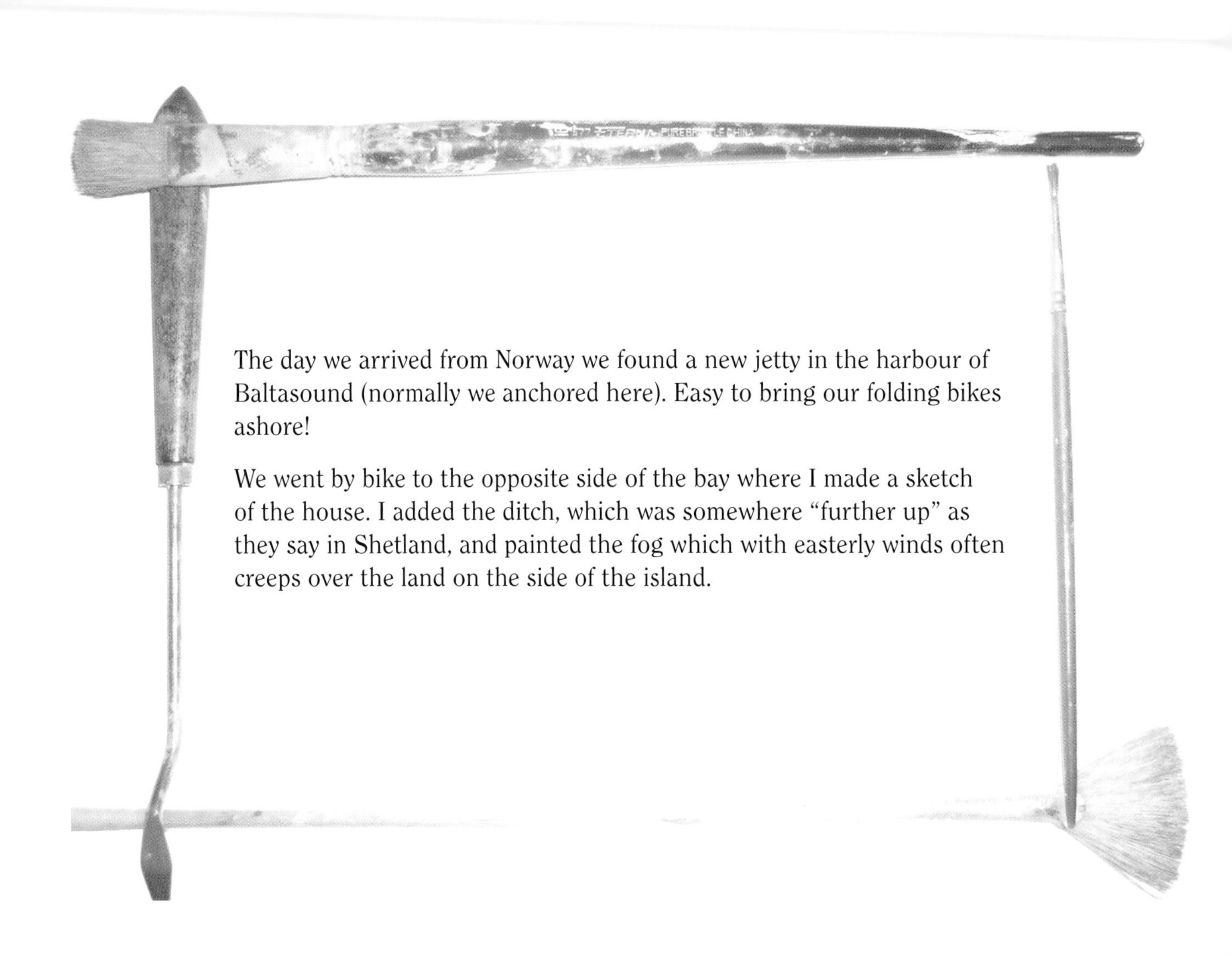

The day we arrived from Norway we found a new jetty in the harbour of Baltasound (normally we anchored here). Easy to bring our folding bikes ashore!

We went by bike to the opposite side of the bay where I made a sketch of the house. I added the ditch, which was somewhere "further up" as they say in Shetland, and painted the fog which with easterly winds often creeps over the land on the side of the island.

Baltasound - Unst

Fishing vessel in Lunning Sound

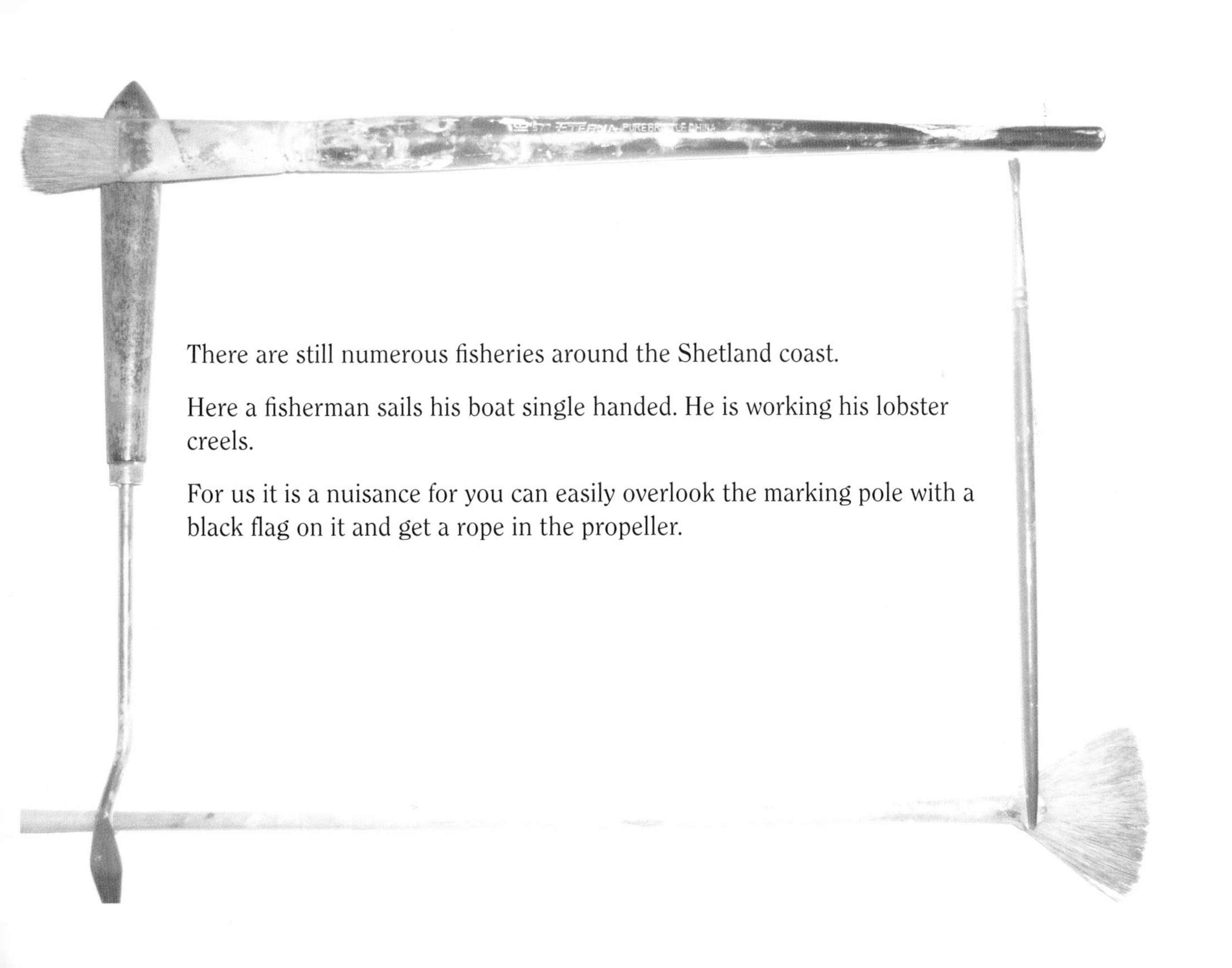

There are still numerous fisheries around the Shetland coast.

Here a fisherman sails his boat single handed. He is working his lobster creels.

For us it is a nuisance for you can easily overlook the marking pole with a black flag on it and get a rope in the propeller.

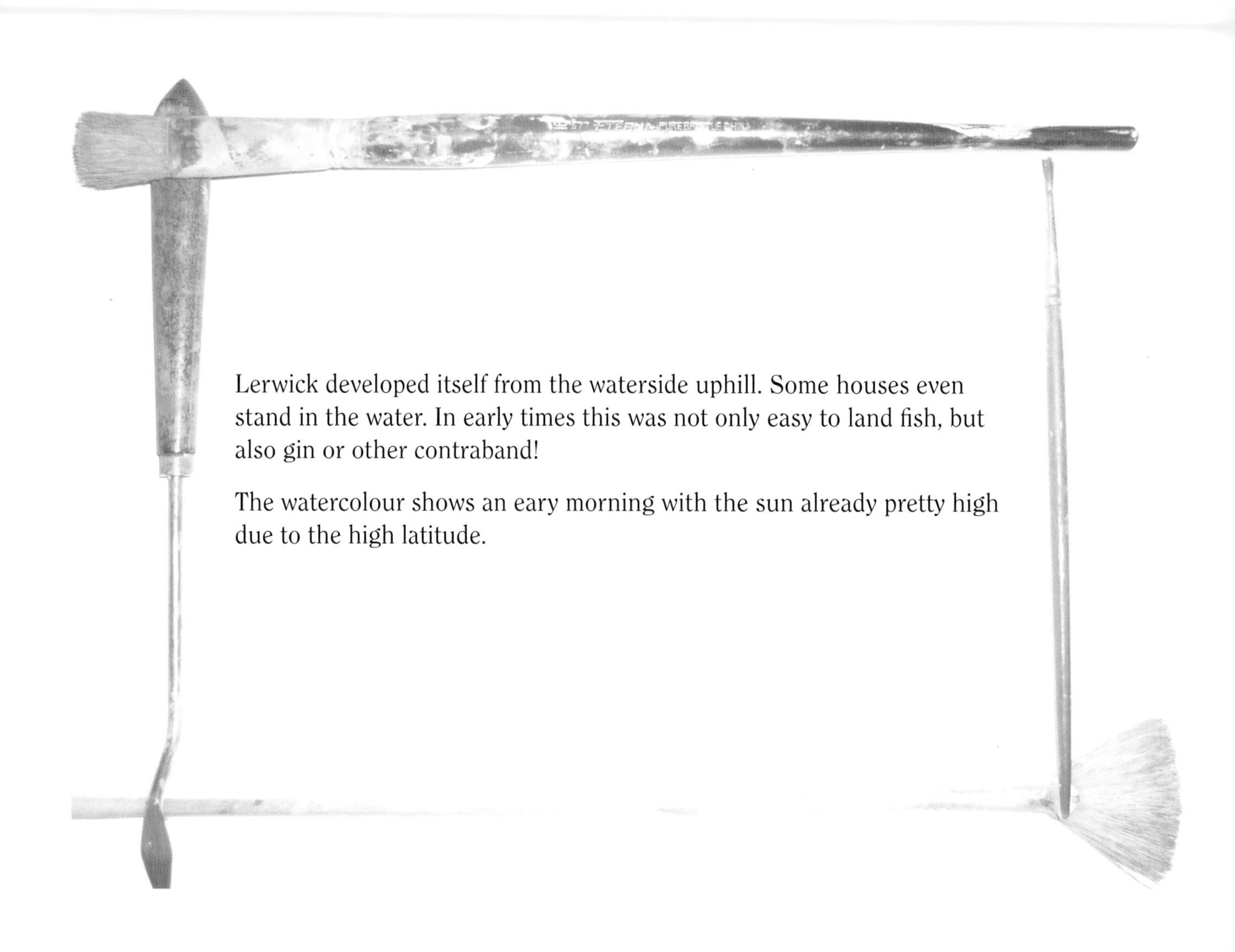

Lerwick developed itself from the waterside uphill. Some houses even stand in the water. In early times this was not only easy to land fish, but also gin or other contraband!

The watercolour shows an eary morning with the sun already pretty high due to the high latitude.

The Lodberrie – Lerwick

Out Skerries

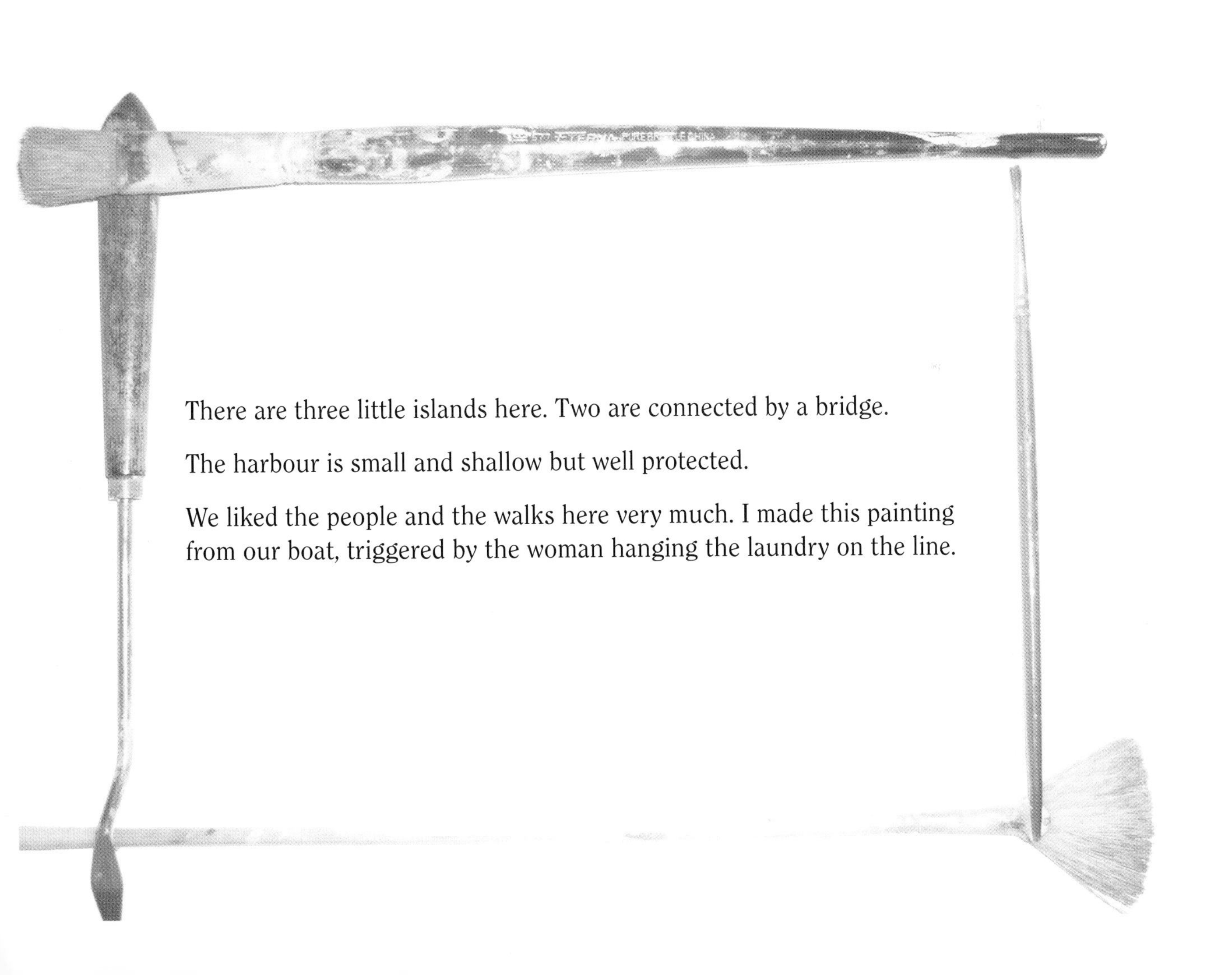

There are three little islands here. Two are connected by a bridge.

The harbour is small and shallow but well protected.

We liked the people and the walks here very much. I made this painting from our boat, triggered by the woman hanging the laundry on the line.

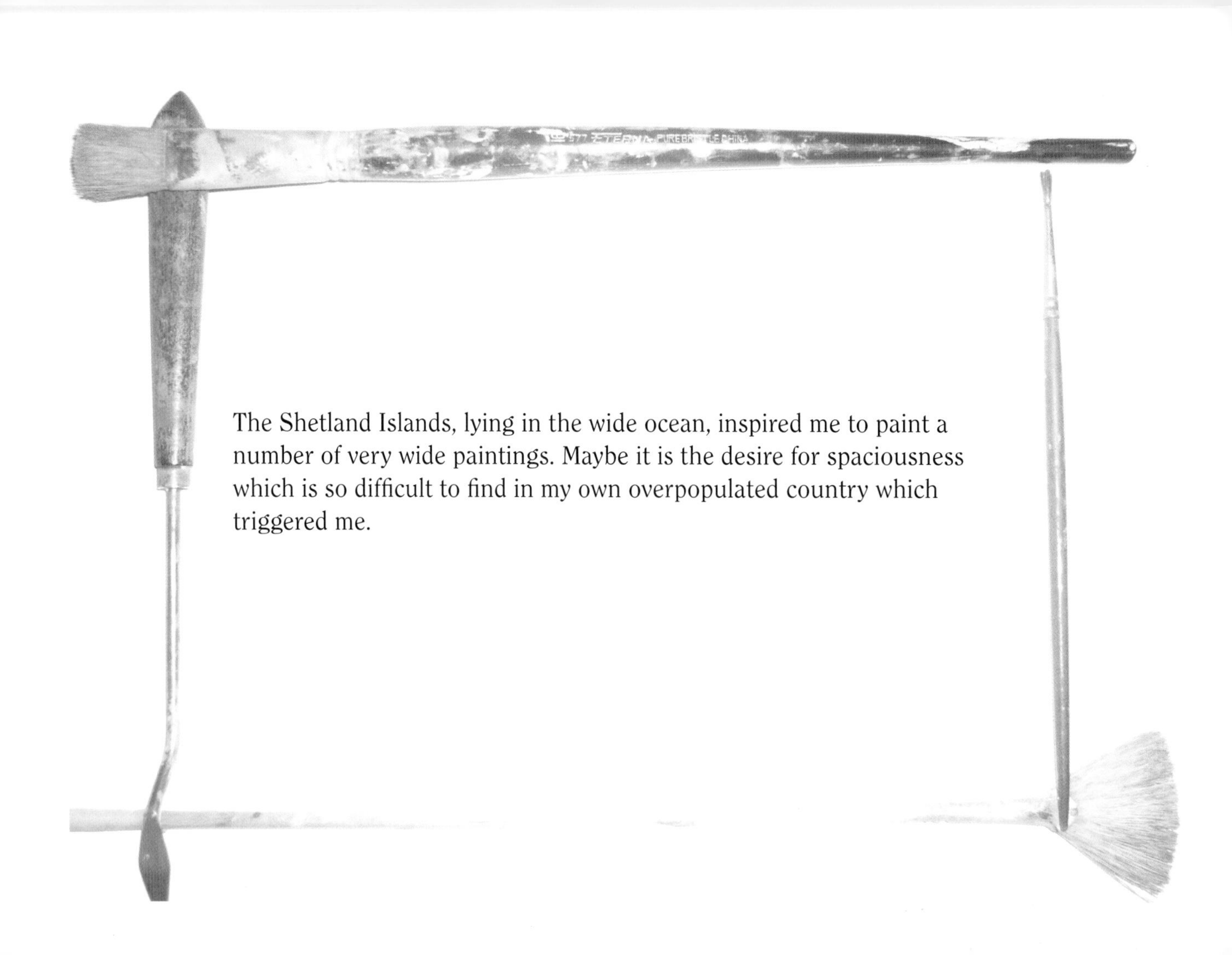

The Shetland Islands, lying in the wide ocean, inspired me to paint a number of very wide paintings. Maybe it is the desire for spaciousness which is so difficult to find in my own overpopulated country which triggered me.

Gunnister - Aith Voe - Bressay

Bigton - South Mainland

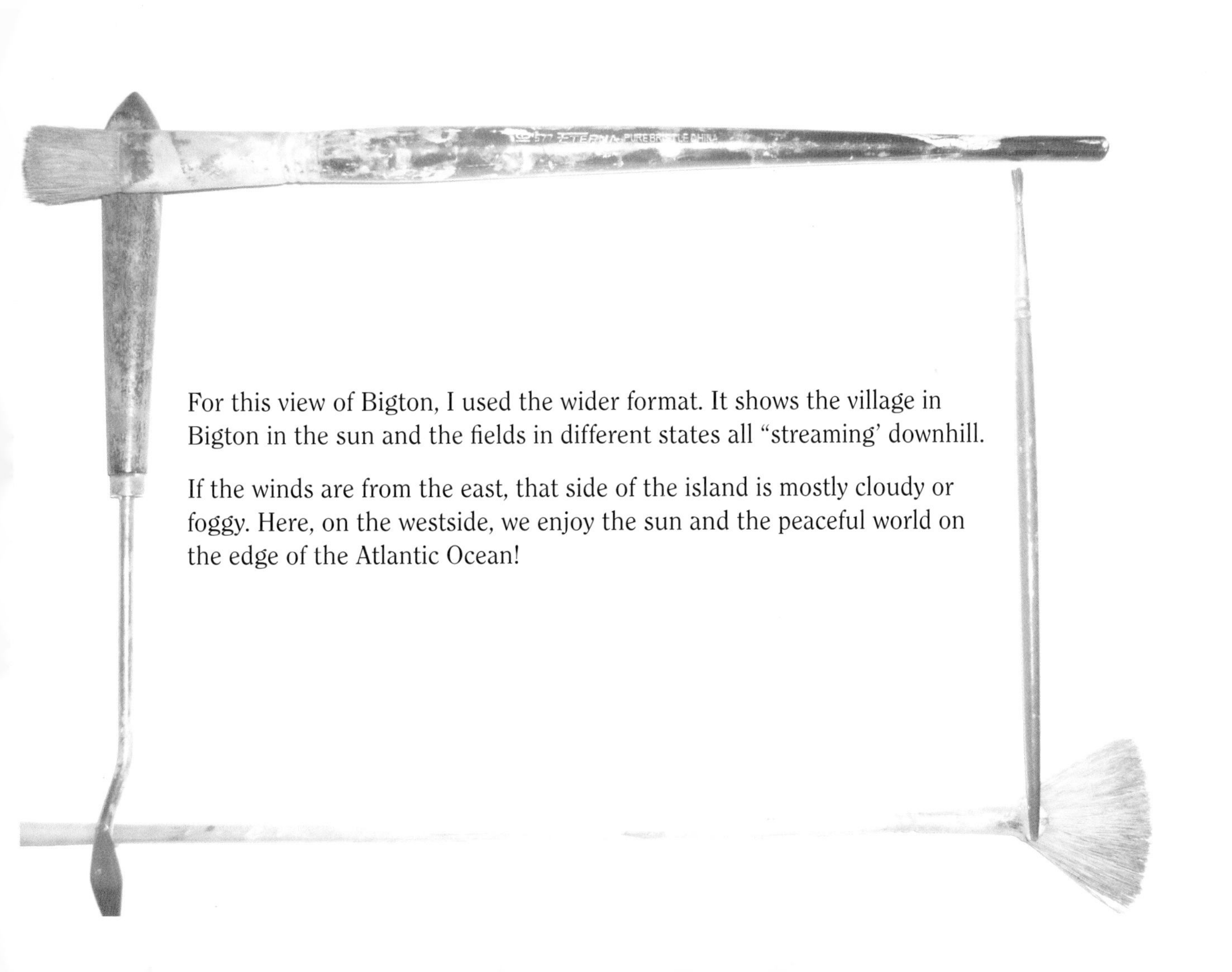

For this view of Bigton, I used the wider format. It shows the village in Bigton in the sun and the fields in different states all “streaming’ downhill.

If the winds are from the east, that side of the island is mostly cloudy or foggy. Here, on the westside, we enjoy the sun and the peaceful world on the edge of the Atlantic Ocean!

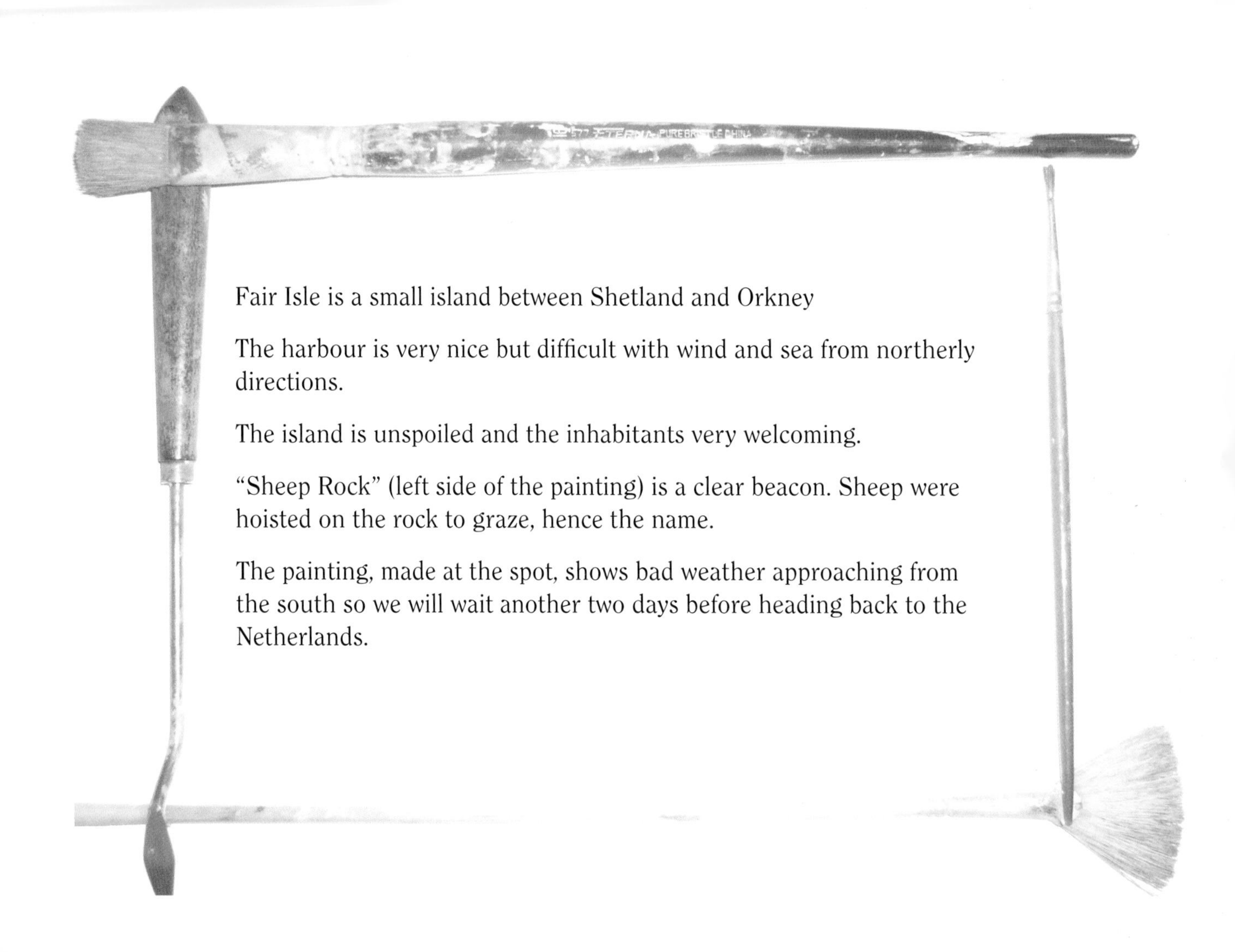

Fair Isle is a small island between Shetland and Orkney

The harbour is very nice but difficult with wind and sea from northerly directions.

The island is unspoiled and the inhabitants very welcoming.

"Sheep Rock" (left side of the painting) is a clear beacon. Sheep were hoisted on the rock to graze, hence the name.

The painting, made at the spot, shows bad weather approaching from the south so we will wait another two days before heading back to the Netherlands.

Fair Isle - Shetland

Dick at work on the pier at Burravoe